11a

CYCLES IN SCIENCE

EARTH

PETER D. RILEY

Heinemann
LIBRARY

First published in Great Britain by Heinemann Library
Halley Court, Jordan Hill, Oxford OX2 8EJ
a division of Reed Educational and Professional Publishing Ltd.
Heinemann is a registered trademark of Reed Educational &
Professional Publishing Limited.

OXFORD FLORENCE PRAGUE MADRID ATHENS
MELBOURNE AUCKLAND KUALA LUMPUR SINGAPORE TOKYO
IBADAN NAIROBI KAMPALA JOHANNESBURG GABORONE
PORTSMOUTH NH CHICAGO MEXICO CITY SAO PAULO

Designed by Visual Image
Illustrations by Visual Image
Printed in Hong Kong

02 01 00 99 98
10 9 8 7 6 5 4 3 2 1

ISBN 0 431 08432 7

British Library Cataloguing in Publication Data

Riley, Peter, 1947-
   The spinning earth. – (Cycles in science)
   1.Earth - Rotation - Juvenile literature 2.Time - Juvenile
   literature 3.Biological rhythms - Juvenile literature
   I.Title
   525.3'5

Acknowledgements

The Publishers would like to thank the following for
permission to reproduce photographs:
Bruce Coleman: S Rosemann p22; T Clifford p10;
Planet Earth Pictures: Aden Jones p5; SPL: p6, G
Garradd p7, D Hardy p8, NASA p9, 15, 16, 29, F
Sauze p12, J Sanford p18, S Fraser p19, D Parker p20,
F Gohier p25, Science Photo Library p28; Space
Telescope Science Institute/NASA p26, 27; SPW:
Chris Butler p4, NASA p24; Tony Stone Images: T
Walker p11, R Smith p14, J Drake p23; TRIP: J
Stanley p21.

Cover photograph reproduced with permission of
David Nunuk, Science Photo Library.

Our thanks to Jim Drake for his comments in the
preparation of this book.

Every effort has been made to contact copyright
holders of any material reproduced in this book. Any
omissions will be rectified in subsequent printings if
notice is given to the Publisher.

Any words appearing in the text in bold, **like
this**, are explained in the Glossary.

CONTENTS

EARTH

If you sat outside from one day to the next without falling asleep, you would notice many changes. In the sky, the Sun would sink, the sky would go dark, the stars would shine, then the sky would brighten and the Sun would rise. During this time you would feel warm, then cold and then warm again. Around you birds would stop flying as night approached and bats would begin to flutter overhead. At dawn birds would sing and fly again. These are just a few of the changes due to the spinning of the Earth.

The sky we see from Earth is really the **atmosphere**. It scatters sunlight into all the colours of the rainbow. Blue light is scattered most which makes the sky look blue. Clouds are water droplets in the atmosphere which reflect sunlight and appear white.

HOW FAST ARE YOU SPINNING?

You are sitting on a ball of rock that weighs nearly 6000 million million million tonnes. It is turning so fast that if you were to stand at the **equator** you would be moving at over 1560 kilometres every hour. The turning speed is slower nearer the North and South **Poles**. All parts of the Earth spin together but places at the equator have much further to travel than places nearer the poles, because of the shape of the Earth. But wherever you are, you are probably moving faster than a racing car.

WHEN DID THE SPINNING START?

Scientists believe that in this part of the universe, about 5 billion years ago, there was a cloud of gas and dust. It stretched for up to 2 million million kilometres in all directions. A star close by exploded. The explosion sent **shock waves** through the gas and dust and started the cloud turning. It formed a flat spinning disc. At the centre a star formed. It was the Sun. Then 4600 million years ago the gas and dust around the Sun gradually joined together to form the planets, including the Earth. As the planets formed they continued to spin in two ways – they spun like **gyroscopes** and they spun round the Sun. They may continue to spin for billions of years to come.

This picture shows how the Earth may have formed. The dust grains joined together to form lumps of rock. The rocks crashed into each other and stuck together to form a rocky planet.

EARLY IDEAS

The Greeks thought that the Sun, Moon, planets and stars were held in different spheres made from a strong, transparent crystal substance. The crystal spheres moved these objects in the sky in circular paths around the Earth. Each sphere moved at its own pace.

The changes in the sky have always fascinated people. There have been many ways of explaining them.

A SKY FULL OF GODS

A dazzling bright ship carrying a god sails across the sky all day and makes it light. After dark, twinkling lights in the sky make pictures of other gods and objects found on Earth. If you had lived a few thousand years ago these ideas would not have seemed strange. People did not see the objects in the sky for what they really are – the Sun, the stars and the planets.

ODD IDEAS

Some ancient people believed the Earth was like a disc floating in a sea. Others thought it was carried by a turtle or elephants. The Romans thought that the god Atlas carried the Earth on his shoulders. Almost everyone believed the Earth to be the centre of the universe.

A NEVER-CHANGING UNIVERSE

There are changes on the Earth like the weather and the seasons but the Ancient Greeks believed that in the heavens nothing changed.

When a **comet** appeared in the sky it was thought to be a part of the **atmosphere**, like a cloud, because the atmosphere was part of the Earth where changes could occur.

A CHANGE OF MIND

In 1543 a Polish **astronomer** called Nicolaus Copernicus published his studies on the heavens and the planets. His measurements of the paths of the planets suggested that they moved round the Sun.

Then in 1577 Tycho Brahe, a Danish astronomer, worked out the measurements of a large comet. They showed that the comet was further away than the Moon and so was outside the atmosphere. The measurements also showed the comet to be moving through space where the crystal spheres were thought to be.

Comets like this one appear in the sky occasionally and move in a path around the Sun that takes them between the planets. Tiny **particles** rush out from the Sun in all directions. They form the solar wind. As the comet gets near the Sun the solar wind blows gas and dust from the comet into two tails. The gas tail is longer than the dust tail.

MODERN IDEAS

The invention of the telescope led to many discoveries about the planets. The most important one was that they did not move round the Earth. The force that holds them in space was worked out by watching an apple fall from a tree.

A CLOSER LOOK AT THE SKY

In 1609 the Italian scientist Galileo built a telescope. When he used it to look at Jupiter he saw four objects he thought were nearby stars. He looked at Jupiter every night for over a month and found that the stars moved to different places around the planet. Eventually, he realised the stars were really moons moving round Jupiter. This discovery showed that everything in the sky did not move round the Earth.

To the naked eye, Venus looks like a ball of light in the night sky. When Galileo examined it with his telescope he found that it had a shiny shape which changed rather like the Moon. These changes suggested that the planet was reflecting light as it moved around the Sun.

This photograph was taken in 1968 by the first astronauts to travel round the Moon. It shows the Moon's cratered surface and the Earth in space held in position by **gravity**.

The **Solar System** is the name given to the Sun and all the planets, **asteroids** and **comets** that move round it. The planets are shown close together here but are really millions of kilometres apart. Pluto is nearly 6000 million kilometres from the Sun.

GOING ROUND IN CIRCLES

In 1609 the German **astronomer**, Johannes Kepler, studied measurements of the movements of the planets. They showed that the planets did not move in a perfect circle round the Sun. He calculated that each planet moved round the Sun in an **elliptical** path that we now call its **orbit**.

Kepler worked out that planets nearer the Sun travelled faster than those further away. The Sun seemed to have some power over the planets but what was it? Kepler and Galileo thought that the Sun and the planets had some magnetic force between them. It was fifty years later that Isaac Newton solved the problem after watching an apple fall off a tree. He thought that the force which pulled the apple to the ground also pulled on the Moon and so made it travel round the Earth. After more thought he realised that a similar force made the planets go round the Sun. This force is gravity.

THE MISSING PLANETS

Mercury, Venus, Mars, Jupiter and Saturn can be easily seen with the naked eye from the Earth. After telescopes were invented, Uranus was discovered in 1781 followed by Neptune in 1846 and Pluto in 1930.

POLES OF THE PLANET

The Earth spins around an imaginary rod which runs right through the planet. The Earth has two sets of poles: the geographic North and South Poles and the magnetic North and South Poles.

A SPINNING SUN

Never look directly at the sun. It can damage your eyes.

People did not know where they were 400 years ago. It seemed that they were no longer at the centre of the universe. They were moving round the Sun. At that time the **astronomer** Galileo also observed that the Sun has spots. He watched them regularly for many days and saw that they move to one side of the Sun, disappear and then re-appear on the other side. He suggested that this was because the Sun was spinning round. He also thought that the Earth was spinning too.

FLYING BACKWARDS

This globe shows the way the Earth tilts on its **axis**.

The idea of a spinning Earth put most people's minds in a spin. They imagined that if the Earth was really spinning then when a bird took to the air it would be left behind or it would fly backwards. They did not believe the Earth could be turning.

SWINGING AND SPINNING

Jean Léon Foucault, a French scientist, studied the to and fro movement of pendulums. He noticed that they always kept swinging in the same direction. He set up a pendulum over 60 metres long and put a spike on the pendulum weight. This made a groove in the sand as the pendulum swung. Although Foucault started the pendulum swinging in a North-South direction he saw a number of grooves were being made by it.

The pendulum was still swinging in a North–South direction so he concluded that the changes were due to the slowly turning Earth.

THE CENTRE OF SPIN

The Earth spins around an imaginary rod which runs right through the planet. The rod is called the **axis** and its ends are the North and South Poles. The Earth has two sets of poles: the geographic North and South Poles and the magnetic North and South Poles. The North Pole is on the ice that covers the Arctic Ocean and the South Pole is on the snow-covered continent of Antarctica. The Earth does not spin straight up and down on its geographic North–South axis but is tilted at an angle of 23$\frac{1}{2}$° from an imaginary vertical line. This makes the Earth appear to lean to one side.

The magnetic force field reaches out into space. Tiny **particles** spraying out from the Sun are directed by the force field to the polar regions where they make a glittering display called an **aurora** as they rush into the **atmosphere**.

THE MEGA-MAGNET

At the centre of the Earth is a very hot liquid of iron and nickel. This moves slowly and makes a magnetic **force field** around the planet. It is as if a giant bar magnet lies inside the Earth. The poles of this magnet do not point to the exact North and South Poles.

TIME ZONES

What is the time? The chances are you will only be a few minutes wrong with your guess. We are very aware of time but in the past, time did not matter as much to people. When towns and cities grew and people could travel quickly between countries, knowing the time everywhere became more important.

TIME – THE ORGANIZER

For the earliest people there were two divisions of time: daytime and night-time. Daytime was the time to hunt and collect fruits and roots. If people wanted to know how much of the day was left they looked to see if the Sun was rising or sinking in the sky. Night-time was the time to sleep.

As the Earth spins round the shadow will move across the sundial.

As people developed, they needed to measure time more accurately so that they could organize their lives. For example, they needed to know the time to meet together for work.

OLD TIMERS

The first invention for measuring time was the **sundial**. It measured the length and direction of a shadow cast by an upright rod. When the day was cloudy or when it was night, a clepsydra or water clock was used. This was like a large bucket with markings on its sides and a small hole in the bottom. As water dripped out the time passing was measured by the changing position of the water level. The sundial and clepsydra were invented 2000–3000 years ago. Clocks have been used for about 600 years.

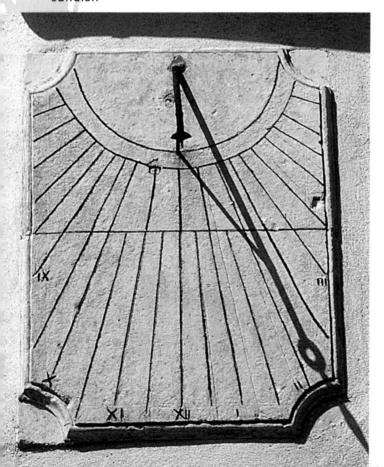

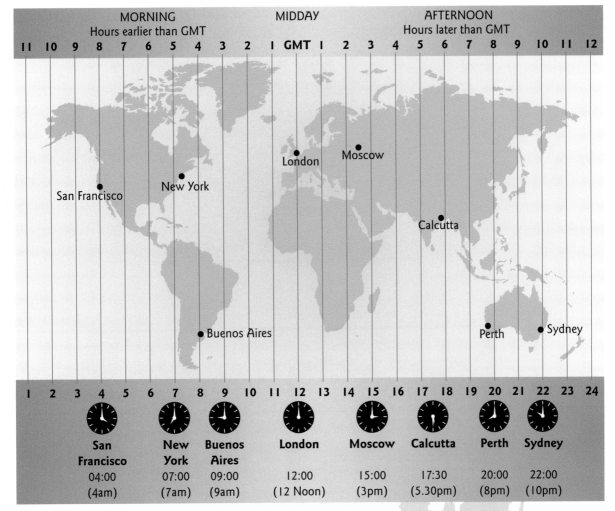

	San Francisco	New York	Buenos Aires	London	Moscow	Calcutta	Perth	Sydney
	04:00 (4am)	07:00 (7am)	09:00 (9am)	12:00 (12 Noon)	15:00 (3pm)	17:30 (5.30pm)	20:00 (8pm)	22:00 (10pm)

TIME ZONES

At first, all towns kept their own time. When people travelled from one town to another they did so by walking or by riding a horse. The journey could take a few hours or even days. When the travellers arrived, they simply changed to using the time in the new town.

When railways were built across continents, people could travel over long distances more quickly. It became important to organize a whole world-wide system of time zones so that all the towns in the same region had the same time.

The Earth is divided into 24 time zones. When you move east into the next time zone you move your watch forward one hour. When you move west you move your watch back one hour.

GRAVITY

*There is a force of attraction between any two objects in the universe. It is called **gravity**. Gravity makes it difficult for us to leave this planet but makes it easy for **black holes** to swallow stars.*

The roller-coaster cars are being pulled to the Earth's surface. The steep slope of the track lets the passengers feel what it is like to almost fall – then brings them down safely.

THE EARTH AND YOU

The size of the force between two objects depends on how much **mass** each object has and how close together they are. The Earth is a massive object and it is very close to you. When you jump you leave the Earth's surface but the Earth's gravity is so strong it pulls you back straight away.

ESCAPING GRAVITY'S GRIP

If you throw a ball in the air, as hard as you can, you will see the ball move from your hand at great speed and then slow down as it gets to its highest point. It then stops and falls back down.

Gravity slowed down the ball and pulled it back. Spacecraft have to be punched into the sky at a speed of 40, 000 kilometres per hour, to reach an **orbit** where they do not fall back to Earth.

STAYING IN SPACE

A spacecraft in orbit is still pulled by gravity but it does not fall because it is travelling at great speed. At 200 kilometres above the Earth a spacecraft must travel at 28,000 kilometres per hour to keep in its orbit. At this speed it falls around the Earth instead of onto it. If the spacecraft travelled faster it would fly off into space.

STARS AND BLACK HOLES

More than 99% of all the mass in the Solar System is in the Sun. The force of gravity of this massive body keeps the planets moving in their orbits and stops them drifting away into space.

When a star three times the size of the Sun comes to the end of its life it may collapse to form an object with such a powerful force of gravity that even light cannot escape. This object is a **black hole**. Its gravity can rip away parts of nearby stars and send them spinning round the black hole before they disappear into it.

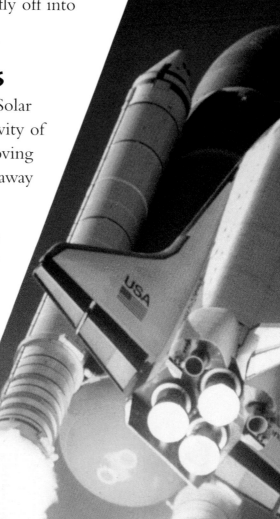

The space shuttle orbiter is fastened to a tank of fuel and two rockets which will provide the energy to push the spacecraft away from the pull of gravity.

THE SPINNING SKY

The Sun and stars were once used for measuring time and finding the positions of ships on the sea. Now satellites are used by sailors, earth scientists and astronomers.

THE CLOCK IN THE SKY

Think of the night sky as a clock face that slowly turns above your head. In the northern **hemisphere** the centre of the clock face is a star called Polaris (the North Star). It is almost directly above the North Pole. In the northern sky is a constellation of stars known as the Plough, Big Dipper or Ursa Major. It looks like a saucepan with a long handle. The Plough can be thought of as the clock hand but it moves in an anti-clockwise direction. So, it is possible to tell the time at night by looking at the position of the stars. In the southern sky a star near the centre of the clock face is Sigma Octantis. It is much dimmer than Polaris. One of the brightest constellations in the southern sky is the Southern Cross. The stars are not actually moving. It is the spinning Earth that makes them look as if they change positions.

The **sextant** is used to measure the angle between a star and the horizon.

FINDING YOUR WAY

In the past, sailors used the Sun and a clock to find out if they were east or west of the port they had left. They found the midday time by noting when the Sun was at its highest in the sky and then read the clock which was keeping the time of the port.

For example, if the home port time was 2 pm the sailors knew the ship was to the west of the port as the Sun had already passed over it. If the home port time was only 11.00 am the sailors knew the ship was east of the port because the Sun had yet to pass over it.

SPOT ON

Today eighteen satellites **orbit** the Earth in **elliptical** orbits to tell people precisely where they are. Sailors can find the position of their ships at any time by switching on a special communicator. Pilots can use the satellites too. They give the position of the aircraft and its height above the Earth's surface.

The Hubble space telescope being repaired by astronauts from the space shuttle.

SPACE JAM

There are hundreds of satellites in orbit around the Earth today. They provide us with weather information, the condition of rainforests and grasslands, the likelihood of earthquakes and can transmit television programmes. The Hubble space telescope is a satellite which points into space to collect information about the universe without the Earth's cloudy **atmosphere** getting in the way.

THE MOON

The Moon is closer to Earth than any other object in space. It is very different from the Earth and has a powerful effect on the oceans' waters.

MOON FACTS

The Moon is about 384,622 kilometres from the Earth and is moving away from us at the rate of 4 centimetres a year. It does not shine with its own light but reflects light from the Sun. The amount of light it reflects changes every night because the Moon is spinning in an **orbit** too. The Moon's orbit takes it around the Earth in 29 1/2 days. During this time it spins round once on its **axis**. This means that the Moon always keeps the same side facing the Earth.

THE MOON'S FACE

The white regions on the Moon are mountains and the grey regions are dusty plains. The circular shapes are craters made by rocks hitting the surface 4000 million years ago. As the Moon's **gravity** is too weak to hold an **atmosphere** there has been no wind or rain to **erode** the rocky crater walls, so they have remained as they were when they first formed.

The changing areas of the moon lit by the Sun are called phases. By looking at the Moon on two nights close together you can tell where the Moon is on its journey round the Earth.

ALL WASHED UP

The force of the Moon's gravity pulls on the water in the Earth's oceans and makes low and high tides. The pull of the Moon's gravity raises the height of the water level in the ocean below it which makes a high tide that covers the shores. On the opposite side of the Earth a similar high tide occurs and between the two sides the water level falls, bringing a low tide. As the Earth spins, another region of the ocean comes under the influence of the Moon's gravity and high tide occurs. It is then low tide where it was high tide before.

As the Moon moves round the Earth it changes position in the sky. This means that the high and low tides do not occur at the same time at the same place every day. Each tide is 12 hours and 25 minutes later than the last.

At low tide the seaweed growing on this rocky shore are exposed to the air. When the tide rises they are covered with water again.

ALL IN A YEAR

The movement of the Earth around the Sun and the movement of the Moon around the Earth are used for measuring time.

MOVING ROUND THE SUN

The Earth is moving round the Sun at 10,400 kilometres per hour. In the time it takes you to read this sentence the Earth will have moved 14 kilometres through space. As the planet makes one complete journey round the Sun it spins 365 1/4 times on its **axis**. During this journey the axis remains tilted in the same direction so that for part of the year the northern **hemisphere** is tilted towards the Sun then the southern hemisphere takes over.

These stones were placed in a ring by people living near Stonehenge in England, a few thousand years ago. It was built to help them measure time from the way the Sun and stars seemed to move in the sky.

MEASURING IN MOONTHS

The regular changes of the Moon are easy to see. Our ancestors used them to measure seasons and years. The time between each new moon is 29 1/2 days so each season is about three 'moonths' or months long. There was a problem with measuring a year in lunar months – the number of days just do not add up. There are 29 1/2 × 12 = 354 days in a year of lunar months but it takes the Earth 11 days longer to make a complete **orbit** round the Sun.

HOW TIMES CHANGED

The Egyptians also noted the positions of the Sun on the horizon and realised it could be used to measure time. They set up a calendar of twelve thirty-day months and added five feast days to celebrate the annual flooding of the River Nile. This gave them a 365-day year. Later civilizations added the extra days to some of the months. The problem of what to do with the quarter day was not solved until 1582 when Pope Gregory decreed that every fourth year, called a leap year, should have an extra day except for years that end in two zeros.

This is the sun shining on a city in the Arctic at midnight! When a **pole** is tilted towards the Sun there is no sunset, just daylight for 24 hours every day for a few months. At the other pole it is permanent night.

LIFE ON A SPINNING PLANET

The tilt of the planet brings seasonal changes to most living things.

THE SEASONS

The Sun's rays bring light and heat to the planet. Land and sea at the **equator** receive a constant amount all year round but to the north and south the amount varies with the time of year. When a **pole** is tilted towards the Sun the **hemisphere** around it receives more light and heat and it is summer there. When the pole is tilted away from the Sun the hemisphere around it receives less light and heat and it is winter there. At the poles there are just these two seasons because conditions change very quickly, but towards the **tropics** the land and sea have two more seasons. The conditions change more slowly in the tropics and the period of warming up between winter and summer is called spring and the period of cooling down between summer and winter is called autumn.

In winter the Earth's **axis** points away from the Sun. Thick coats keep the deer warm.

ALL CHANGE

Spring and autumn are the seasons of greatest change. In spring the amount of heat and light increases. The heat warms the soil and makes the seeds sprout. Tree buds burst into leaf, insects hatch from eggs and **pupa,** and larger animals prepare to breed.

In the autumn, broad-leaved trees shed their leaves as they will not be able to draw water from the frozen ground during the winter season that follows. Many adult insects die but others survive by sheltering until the spring. Insect-eating bats find little to eat so they hibernate. Insect-eating birds, like the swallow, migrate to warmer places where they can still catch food.

HIGH ENERGY DAYS OF SUMMER

Light and heat are forms of energy. Plants trap some of the light energy in their leaves. They use the energy to make food to keep themselves alive, to grow and make seeds. The heat energy speeds up the way they make food and grow. The heat also helps young animals keep warm as they grow. The plants provide food for many animals. Some animals gorge themselves to grow fat which they will use up during the winter when there is little food to find.

PREPARING FOR THE WORST

Bears prepare for winter by eating large amounts of food and making body fat. They use the energy in fat to keep them alive while they hibernate. Desert frogs in Australia prepare for the dry season by filling themselves up with so much water that they are almost shaped like a ball.

In summer the Earth's axis points towards the Sun. Plants grow fast in the light and warmth, and provide food for many animals. It is the time when animals breed and rear their young.

23

SPINNING TO DISASTER

There are rocks in space that may hit the Earth with devastating results.

WHY ARE THERE ASTEROIDS?

When the planets formed there was some cosmic dust left over and it swirled around the Sun. The specks of dust joined together to form chunks of rock and these collected and formed huge **boulders** in space. If all these rocks and boulders had joined together they would have formed a planet more than 30 times smaller than the size of the Moon, but Jupiter's powerful force of **gravity** has kept them scattered in space.

Gaspra is the first asteroid to be photographed from a passing **space probe**. It is 12 kilometres long and spins so fast that a day on it would only take seven hours.

A ROCKY BELT

Most of the pieces of rock, ranging in size from a few millimetres to over 900 kilometres long, move around the Sun between the **orbits** of Mars and Jupiter. They form a belt of **rubble** about 200 million kilometres from the Earth which stretches for 150,000 kilometres towards Jupiter. So far, over 10,000 of these **asteroids** have been identified.

COMING CLOSER

Some asteroids have orbits that cross the orbit of the Earth. These asteroids are known as Apollo asteroids. In 1996 an asteroid called 1996JA1, measuring between 300 – 500 metres and weighing about 150 million tonnes, passed within 448,000 kilometres of the Earth.

METEORS

Meteors are small pieces of space rock that came from the dust in comets' tails or the dust cloud that formed the **Solar System**. Like all pieces of space rock they travel at up to 40 kilometres per second. When they rush into the Earth's **atmosphere** they rub against the **particles** in the air and friction makes them heat up and glow. Each meteor leaves a streak of light in the sky. They break up into dust before reaching the Earth.

METEORITES

A piece of space rock weighing about the same as an apple racing through the atmosphere is too big to burn up completely and falls to the ground. Space rocks which reach the ground are called meteorites. They may come from an asteroid or be a piece of the Moon or Mars that has been thrown into space after impact with an asteroid. Some meteorites may be the rocky parts of **comets**.

This crater was made by a meteorite that weighed more than 38 jumbo jets.

A STAR'S LIFE

A star is not a living thing but it has stages which are very much like those in a life cycle.

THE MOVING SUN

The Sun is a yellow star. It is so large that over a million planets the size of the Earth could fit inside it. It spins on its **axis** once every 24 days 16 hours. The Sun is turning in a circle too. It is just one of 500 million stars which form the Milky Way **galaxy** in which our Solar System lies. This huge star group is shaped like a wheel and is 100,000 **light years** across. The galaxy also turns like a wheel so every star revolves around its centre. The Sun with its planets around it takes 225 million years to make the journey.

A view through the Hubble space telescope showing stars and **galaxies**. The faint blue galaxies are three to eight billion light years away. They appear blue because large numbers of stars are forming in them.

THE LIFE CYCLE OF A STAR

A star forms from part of a dust cloud called a **nebula**. It is made from hydrogen, helium and dust. They are pulled together by gravity. Eventually, the hydrogen begins to change into helium and the star starts to shine.

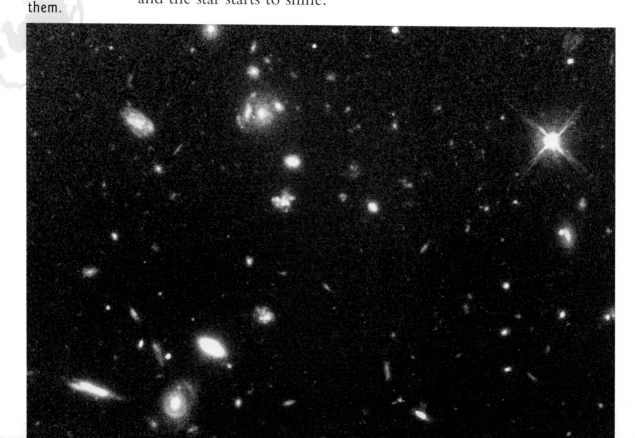

The star may
shine without
much change
for 10,000
million years, if
it is the size of
the Sun but
larger stars have
shorter lives.

As the hydrogen store
of a Sun-sized star gets
lower and lower, the star's
core becomes hotter and the
star begins to swell and turn red. It
becomes a red giant star. Eventually the helium
that remains is changed to carbon and the star
periodically shrinks and swells as it releases dust into
space. Towards the end of its life it turns into a white
dwarf star which cools and turns into a black dwarf star
that fades into the blackness of space. Some large stars
explode.

When all the star dust
has scattered from this
supernova explosion, a
neutron star or perhaps a
black hole will be left
behind.

A MESSAGE FROM ALIENS?

In 1967 a regular blip on a radio at an **observatory**
seemed to be coming from aliens in space. It was
eventually discovered to come from a type of neutron star
called a **pulsar**. This star spins round fast sending out a
beam of radio waves like a lighthouse sending out a beam
of light rays. A neutron star forms when a star a little
larger than the Sun collapses.

THE END

As far as we know, the Earth is the only place in the universe where there is life. The end of the Earth could be seen as the time when the planet can no longer provide a home for living things. Here are some ways in which life might end on Earth.

IN THE CLOUDS

The gases and dust from exploding stars form clouds which are so large they could hide many other **solar systems** inside them. As our Solar System spins round with the **galaxy** it could move into a cloud. If it did there could be so many **particles** of dust between Earth and the Sun that they would stop some of the Sun's heat and light reaching the Earth. This would stop plant growth and cool the planet so that most living things could not survive.

The Sun's surface shoots out huge columns of gas and bursts of particles. If very large amounts of gas and particles were released the Earth's **climate** could change.

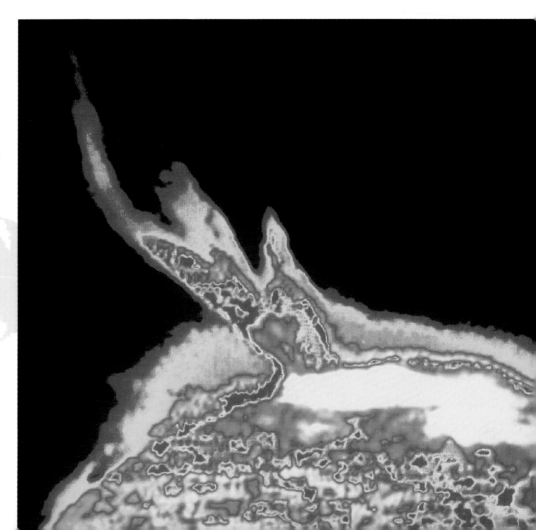

DEATH RAYS

When a star explodes it releases X-rays, **cosmic rays** and **ultraviolet** light. These travel through space and gradually lose their power but a star exploding within 50 **light years** of the Earth could send out deadly rays that would reach our planet.

WHEN THE SUN SWELLS UP

In 5000 million years the Sun's supply of hydrogen will have run out and the star will have swelled into a red giant star. As it swells it will reach the **orbit** of Mercury and swallow the planet. It may reach and swallow Venus too. Although it will not reach the Earth, all life here would perish. At that time the Sun will appear like a huge tomato in the sky shining a thousand times brighter than it does today.

The latest rover examining the surface of Mars. Technology is already well developed to take people from Earth to two of our near neighbours – the Moon and Mars. In a hundred years there may be plans for some people to leave the Solar System for stars with other planets spinning round them.

WHERE WILL WE BE?

A few stars have already been found to have planets and some people say that the chance of finding planets where life can flourish are extremely good. People have already walked on the Moon and there are plans to visit Mars soon. Perhaps in a few generations humans will travel beyond the Solar System and find planets to call home when the Earth does come to an end.

GLOSSARY

asteroid a piece of rock which orbits around the Sun

astronomer a person who studies the stars, the planets and their moons, and other structures in the universe such as gas clouds and black holes

atmosphere the mixture of gases, mainly nitrogen and oxygen, that surrounds the Earth

aurora a bright glow of light in the sky due to charged particles from the Sun rushing into the atmosphere

axis an imaginary rod running through the Earth from pole to pole around which the Earth turns

black hole a region of space formed by the collapse of a large star which has such a strong force that light cannot escape from it

boulder a large rock

climate the weather conditions that occur at a place on earth during the course of a year

comet an icy rock in a very large orbit around the Sun that produces tails of dust and gas as it approaches and leaves the Sun

core the centre of an object such as an apple or a planet

cosmic rays are made of tiny particles that come from the Sun and other stars and move almost at the speed of light

elliptical having an oval shape

equator an imaginary line around the middle of the Earth that is the same distance from each pole

erode to gradually wear away or break up

force field a region in which the effect of a force such as gravity or a magnetic force can be felt

friction a force which is generated when one object rubs against another

galaxy a huge cluster of stars

gravity a force of attraction between any two objects in the universe; its effect is most noticeble between a large and a small object, such as a person and the Earth or between the Sun and the planets

gyroscope a rotating wheel that keeps its balance

hemisphere a half of the Earth either around the North or South Pole

light years the distance travelled by a ray of light in one year: 9.5 million million kilometres

mammal an animal with a skeleton of bone and a skin covered in fur which rears its young on milk in the early stages of their life

mass the amount of matter in a substance such as a solid, liquid or gas

nebula a cloud of dust and gas in space

neutron a particle in an atom which does not have an electrical charge

observatory a place where telescopes are used to study stars, planets and other objects in the universe

orbit the path of a planet around the Sun, a moon around a planet or an artificial satellite around the Earth

particle a very tiny object, such as a grain of sand or even a neutron from inside an atom

pole a place at each end of the Earth's axis around which the stars seem to move as the Earth rotates

pulsar a collapsed star called a neutron star which spins fast and gives out a beam of energy which is received on Earth as pulses as the beam sweeps by

pupa a stage in the life cycle of many insects between the caterpillar and the adult when the insect makes a case in which its changes take place

rubble a collection of rocky fragments

satellite an object which moves around a planet, such as a moon or a machine which orbits the Earth, transmitting television programmes or collecting information about the weather

sextant an instrument used by sailors for measuring the heights of the Sun and the stars above the horizon to help keep their ships on course

shock wave a fast moving change in pressure that is released in an explosion

Solar System the Sun and objects that move around it such as the planets and their moons, asteroids and comets

space probe a machine sent into space to investigate the conditions in other parts of the Solar System

sundial a device for measuring time using the position of the Sun

supernova an exploding star

tropics a region of the Earth on either side of the equator marked by an imaginary line 23° to 27° north and south of the equator

ultraviolet light waves of energy, slightly smaller than light waves but carrying more energy, that can burn skin

INDEX